The Weighver's Seaport

A short history of
Hollingworth Lake Littleborough
from 1790 to the present time

An Account of the Development of The Lake
and how it became known as 'The Weighvers' Seaport;
together with a look at The Surrounding District

Including a Brief Record of Notable Characters
and Unusual and Remarkable Events
which have occurred at the Lake

By A W Colligan JP
in association with George Kelsall
with additional notes by Eleanor Dale

Published by G Kelsall
The Bookshop 22 Church Street Littleborough Lancashire
Text © G Kelsall Second Edition 1998

Designed by Ernest Connell

Printed by Smith Settle, Otley, West Yorkshire.

This book has been written to tell the story of Hollingworth Lake; of how a reservoir built nearly 200 years ago became known as 'The Lake' and at the height of its popularity in Victorian Times, as 'The Weighvers' Seaport'. It is many years since any guide to the Lake was published and it is hoped that this book will provide interest and pleasure for residents and visitors alike and help to show how the Lake has developed into the large social and sporting complex we know today.

In this one small book it can only be possible to give a picture of the life and activity at Hollingworth since 1800; it remains for some scholar to write the full history of this area and the immense changes brought about by the industrial revolution. The details are based mainly on available sources and I hope the book will provide the reader with as much pleasure as I have gained in compiling it.

My thanks are due to Clifford Ogden JP, Eric Percival, George Marsden, Jack Mills, Martin Jackson and many others for personal information given in conversation. Mrs E Ingham provided valuable information on the 'Hollingworth Hero'. Arthur Butterworth and Alan Luke kindly helped with old photographs of the Lake and its surroundings. George Kelsall has assisted with research, and photographs, and taken on all the comings and goings which go into the making of a book of this kind. The Rochdale Librarian, and staff are also thanked for their assistance with old records and photographs.

Care has been taken in assembling quotations and photographs. Apologies are made for any infringement of copyright. Without the benefit of photographs, past and present, such a book would not be possible.

AWC January 1977

The Author
Austin Wm. Colligan comes from a family who have lived in Littleborough for over 150 years. He was formerly Headmaster of St. Joseph's School in Bury. For 28 years he served on the old Littleborough Council, being Chairman on three occasions and also a JP. Since retirement he has devoted much of his leisure time to his interest in local history and topography and is a founder member of the local Archaeological Society, a member of the Local History Society and a Life Member of Littleborough Cricket Club. Hc has given talks on "Old Littleborough" and other subjects and has written two other books, both histories of the Churches in Littleborough;
The Village Church (Littleborough C of E) 1974
Living Still (St Mary's RC Church) 1975

Note to the second edition
This book was first published in 1977 just at the time when Hollingworth Lake was becoming established as a country park. It has been in print almost continuously since then. The author Austin Colligan died in 1982 at the age of 77 and with his passing Littleborough lost a dedicated historian but others continue to research and record our local history with considerable success. For this new printing Eleanor Dale has kindly added a brief recent history of the Lake to bring us to the end of the twentieth century.

A mystery solved
Mr Colligan's writing has stood the test of time but it is worth noting that the Alphabet Stone described on page 31 is in fact located in a private garden not far from the old school.

opposite
Holiday crowd on Lake Bank around the turn of the century

Introduction

For years Hollingworth Lake has been a focus for visitors who know it well and return again and again to enjoy a day in the open air. Yet it will come as a surprise to many people to learn that this small country area, nestling at the foot of the Pennine moors, is rich in history and tradition. A hundred years ago the Lake was the scene of great holiday gatherings when thousands arrived by train and on foot. There is a fine record of sports and sportsmen, while many dramas and tragedies of different kinds have been acted out on and around the Lake. The history of any locality is also the history of its people; those who lived there and those who came to leave their mark in some way. Today, Hollingworth Lake is widely known as a centre for countryside recreation, and since 1975 it has become officially known as a 'Country Park'. On summer weekends activities abound on the water and around the shore, yet other visitors come to enjoy the quiet paths away from the noise and bustle. Indeed, by following these walks a constantly changing view is unfolded - from the distant Lancashire towns, around to the farms and the high moorland ridge of Robin Hood's Bed on Blackstone Edge. Animal, bird and plant life add interest for visitors and provide a wealth of study for the serious naturalist.

To the surprise of many this so called Lake is not really a lake but is a man-made reservoir, which during the last two centuries has become such a part of the local landscape that it appears to be a natural creation.

In order to know why it was made we must look back to the 18th century when great changes came about in industrial working. In Lancashire, textile work previously done in cottages and small hillside water driven mills began to be carried out on a much greater scale in new factories. Steam power was developed to drive the vast numbers of new machines set up in the factories whilst a network of canals was developed to transport the coal and raw materials throughout the area which we now know as the Industrial North of England. At that time goods could only be moved by road or canal, for the railways were not to appear until much later.

This part of Lancashire, set at the foot of the Pennines and rising from 500 feet above sea level in Littleborough to 1550 feet on the crest of the moors and dividing Lancashire from the West Riding of Yorkshire, had one main pass at Summit; that is apart from the crossing over Blackstone Edge. This high moorland range was referred to by Defoe as 'Those Andes of England' and the lady on horseback, C Feinnes, in using the so called 'Roman Road' was reminded of the Alps. There was no route to Todmorden along the present road; this way was impassable due to the low lying marshy ground by the River Roch and the only road went by way of Calderbrook over Reddyshore - Scout Gate and eventually down to Walsden. It is recorded that on this road passengers had often to get out of the coach and push it up the hills, even in good weather. In the Hollingworth and Rakewood area travel was by means of sheepwalks and simple tracks to the farms. So everything called for improved means of communication before industry could develop in this part of Lancashire as it was doing elsewhere.

opposite
Full sail at the Lake with Hollingworth Fold in the background

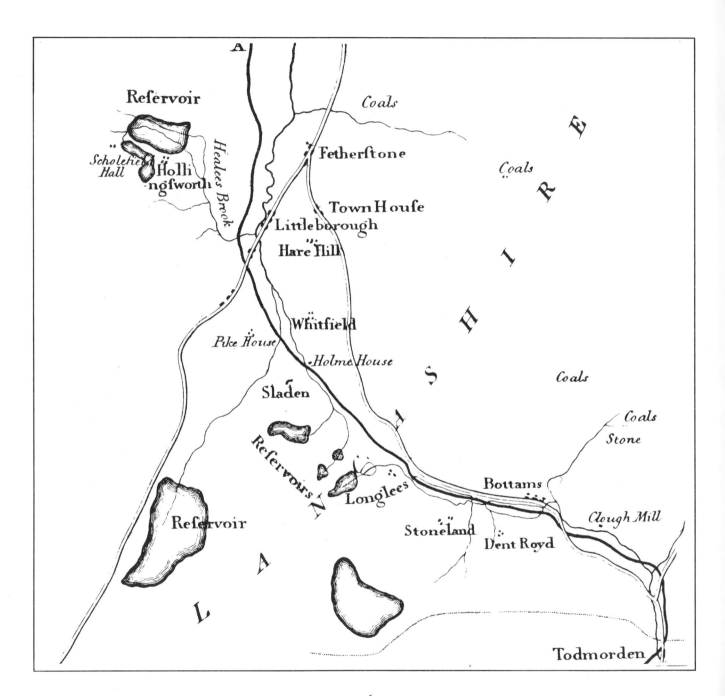

Reservoir

Scholefield
Hall

Holli
ngsworth

Healees Brook

Coals

Fetherstone

Coals

Town House

Littleborough

Hare Hill

Whitfield

Pike House

Holme House

Sladen

Reservoirs

Longlees

Reservoir

Stoneland

Coals

Coals

Stone

Bottams

Clough Mill

Dent Royd

Todmorden

A

S H I R E

L A N

The coming of the Rochdale Canal

During the middle of the 18th Century a feverish spate of canal building was taking place and spreading all over England. There were many difficulties with the early 'navigations' - a word which gave the name 'navvie' to the men who dug them. Often an Appeal to Parliament was made for an Act to establish a new canal; to borrow money for that purpose; to purchase land and to obtain way-leaves and remove local objections. This could be a long drawn out procedure especially if there were legal arguments over land and rights of way. However, if we look at Aikin's book '40 Miles Around Manchester' published in 1795 we see that progress was being made. Aikin tells us:

'The great advantages accruing to trade from water carriage have at all times been known to commercial nations and in proportion, as we in this Island have advanced in manufacture and commerce, plans for connecting the internal parts of the country to the Seaports by navigations have been encouraged and multiplied. It was natural that the use of rivers should be the first expedient for that purpose and many projects of this kind have been brought to effect.'

Aikin mentions the use of rivers and artificial waterways to join up the inland towns to the ports of Manchester and Liverpool thus speeding up the export and import of goods. Details of the Mersey and Irwell navigation go back to 1720 and equally surprising is that Merchants in Leeds had an Act in 1698 for making and keeping navigable the rivers Aire and Calder. In 1740 Halifax merchants engaged Messrs Street and Eyers to survey the Calder and followed this by taking on Smeaton, the famous builder of the Eddystone Lighthouse, to survey from Wakefield to Sowerby Bridge. This resulted in a canal - 'The Aire and Calder Navigation' with 27 locks - being completed on the Yorkshire side of the Pennine Range. By comparison the local 33 miles of canal - 'The Rochdale Canal' stretching from Sowerby Bridge to Manchester - did not arrive until much later.

It was intended that by linking the Rochdale Canal with the Yorkshire one that eventually it would be possible to link Hull and the North Sea with Manchester and Liverpool or as said at the time 'to join the German Ocean to the Irish Sea'. The Rochdale Canal was begun in 1794 and took some ten years to complete, in three stages: Sowerby Bridge to Todmorden - finished in August 1798; Todmorden to Rochdale - December 1798; Rochdale to Manchester 1802. The Rochdale Section, sponsored by local industrialists such as Newall and Beswick of Littleborough, and Fielden of Todmorden, when finished contained 92 locks from Sowerby Bridge to Manchester; together with 6 bridges, 8 aqueducts and a tunnel 70 yards long. The Rochdale Section cost £471,950 in all, raised by shareholders of the Company who had great hopes of financial gain.

For obvious reasons, including cost and labour, the routes of the canals often followed the rivers and the objective of the construction was to keep a good water level in the canal and to avoid interference from natural streams of different origins and water values. Many new and extraordinary contrivances were used to assist the passage of the canals-embankments as at Todmorden Road Littleborough, tunnels as at Stanedge and aqueducts such as the famous one at Barton near Manchester which carried the Bridgewater Canal at a height of 38 feet above the River Irwell.

To keep the flow of water in our local Rochdale Canal, which at Summit is 600 feet above sea level, falling 438 feet to Manchester and 319 feet to Sowerby Bridge - and because of objections to the streams flowing into the Rivers Irk and Irwell being drained to feed the proposed canal - it was decided, and I quote:

'To build great reservoirs in the hilly country near different parts of its course to supply water against all the waste at the locks and also waste by leakage without having to borrow from adjacent streams.'

The final completion of the Rochdale Canal was made when in 1804 an Act of Parliament approved all the above and also covered parts and plans previously not accounted for in the initial stages of planning.

opposite
Aikins map of the Rochdale Canal 1794, showing the proposed Hollingworth Lodge with a smaller reservoir which was never built

To decide on the route of the new canal the Canal Company's surveyors would need to have carried out careful investigations of the land along the way and all the different ownerships. Equally important would have been the search for a suitable site for the new reservoir, large enough to hold sufficient water and not too difficult for the construction of embankments. There is in the Rochdale Library a copy of an old map which appears to show the farmland in the Hollingworth area as it existed in 1793 - one or two local people also have copies of this map. It seems to show the land which the Canal Company's surveyors and engineers expected to flood to make the reservoir and they recorded on the map the names of the owners or tenants of each piece of land (given in the old measure of acres, rods and perches). A modified version of the map is shown here; perhaps the most fascinating part is is what appears to be the proposal for another smaller reservoir on the higher ground between the top of Hollingworth Fold and Schofield Hall. This second lodge was never built for reasons which are now lost to us; maybe there were construction difficulties or financial problems.

			A	R	P
1	Thomas Thornhill Esq	Ben Chadwick	11	3	12
2	Thomas Thornhill Esq	John Kershaw	3	1	31
3	Thomas Thornhill Esq	Thomas Whatmough	5	3	4
4	Thomas Thornhill Esq	Sarah Shore	5	3	34
5	Benjamin Taylor	John Fletcher	5	3	12
6	John Kershaw	Thomas Stott			
7	John Kershaw	William Taylor	1	3	3
8	John Gorrell	Sarah Belfield	32	0	11
9	Edward Kendal	Thomas Hurst	4	0	20
10	Butterworth Poor		5	2	12
11	John Ashworth	Thomas Kershaw	6	1	38
12	John Fazakerly		16	1	12
13	John Fazakerly	Simeon Hurst	4	2	16
14	Simeon Dearden	S. Fielden	6	3	26
15	John Entwisle Esq	James Wild	5	1	13
16	John Entwisle Esq	Robert Howarth	4	2	26
	John Entwistle	Abm Sutcliffe			
17	John Lord	Simeon Hurst	1	2	5
18	Hannah Butterworth		4	0	32
	Lanes & Brooks		1	2	19
			135	3	0

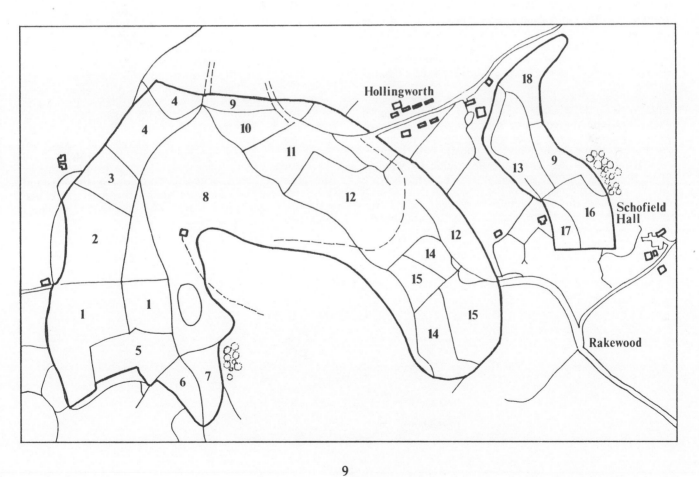

Hollingworth

Schofield
Hall

Rakewood

The reservoirs

To supply the necessary storage of water for the new canal two large lodges or reservoirs were planned - one at Hollingworth covering some 120 acres together with about 40 acres of low lying marshy ground and another, well up on the Blackstone Edge Moors, called Whiteholme of about 90 acres. In fact it was found necessary to build five reservoirs in this area - as recorded by John Sutcliffe in 'A Treatise on Canals and Reservoirs' 1816. No doubt before the engineers selected Hollingworth as the most suitable site for the major reservoir they looked around the other valleys in the area. In Rochdale Library there survives a sketch detail of an earlier proposal of 1792 to build the reservoir in the Ealees Valley which would have covered all the land in the natural hollow over the new car park down to near Lane Foot Farm where presumably there would have been a high dam or embankment.

The making of the Lodge which later became known as Hollingworth Lake meant the flooding of farm land and the covering of a few small buildings. By the way, despite popular legend, there is no church at the bottom of the lake and no ghostly bells ringing. The water to fill the lake came of course by streams from the moors, where catchment water channels were made, and then flowed in by Rakewood as can be seen when crossing the low ground at what is called 'the back of the Lake'. There was no large natural hollow to form a reservoir and so high embankments had to be made on three sides, the main one, 'Hollingworth Bank', being to cut off the Ealees Valley - where the road runs from near the Fisherman's Inn towards Rakewood. The other embankments are 'Fens Bank' which runs from the Fishermans towards the Beach Hotel and 'Shaw Moss Bank' which is on the south side, towards the Navy League.

A full and detailed account of the construction of Hollingworth Lake, the other reservoirs and the Canal would be an interesting and formidable task but one beyond the scope to this little book. There is much for the reader who wishes to look further into this early history in the local libraries and among the pages of some of the books in my bibliography. Sutcliffe, for example, describes how water from the Lake was lifted by steam power and fed into a channel which ran for four miles to supply water to the higher level at Summit Littleborough. This channel can still be seen today, winding its way up to Syke, back to below Whittaker, then to Owlet Hall and eventually up to Summit. The pumping house stood at the back of Bear Hill, Lower Hollingworth and Beckett informs us that the steam powered pumping engine raised the water about 45 feet from the Lake level and into the drain (channel); the engine falling into disuse, being demolished around 1910. Meanwhile let us look at how this man-made lake developed into a well-known and much loved place of pleasure and amusement.

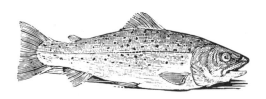

The Lodge was also used to supply water to the new mills which were rapidly developing, both alongside the canal and up the new low level road from Littleborough to Todmorden, popularly called 'Gale Road'. The next great step occured with the coming of the Manchester and Leeds Railway (later to become part of the Lancashire and Yorkshire) in 1839. Today a plaque on the wall of Littleborough Station records the coming of the Railway and the building of the famous tunnel at Summit which was at that time, 1841, the longest railway tunnel in Europe. In Littleborough and roundabout more houses were built as people came to live in the district - some to work at the reservoirs and on the railway, others to work on new buildings. Others came from country districts to work in the new cotton mills and factories. The growth of this district went forward, as did Rochdale and Todmorden, creating a new populace. The Hollingworth Lodge was by this time known as The Lake and became popular as a place to visit during leisure hours - and as workers now finished their week at noon on Saturdays, a walk around the Lake became something of a habit with the locals. It was not long before the possibilities for organised enjoyment and pleasure on a bigger scale began to be realised.

The Rochdale Canal Co leased the use of the Lake, apart from water rights, to two Littleborough men - Henry Newall of Harehill, who owned Harehill Woollen Mills, and his engineer Mr Sladen. Newall, who also owned the new Gasworks, and Sladen, who was soon to take on the landlordship of the Mermaid Inn on the approach to Hollingworth Fold, went to work on pleasure developments on and around the Lake. Boating and novelty amusements were the main attractions. The Lake, which is 2 miles 372 yards round and has an average depth of 30 feet with a suggested depth of 80 feet at the centre was not without its problems.

below and overpage
Advertisements from local Guides printed in Victorian times

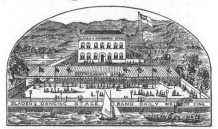

The water is extremely cold and there are under-currents from its various feeds and from the drain going down the Ealees Valley. All the same it soon became popular for boating and a Rowing Club was formed in 1860 and a Regatta followed in 1862. The introduction of two paddle steamers in 1856 and small rowing boats was followed by the building of two outstanding hotels - the 'Beach Hotel' and the 'Lake Hotel and Gardens'. There were hopes of catering for the growth of weekend visitors and day trippers. In those days a full week's holiday away from home was rare and a weekend or day-trip was the popular thing. By the middle of the 19th Century the Railway Company was exploiting the pleasures of the Lake Area and trips by rail were being advertised over a wide area of Lancashire and the West Riding. In fine weather, crowds would arrive by train at Smithybridge and Little-borough Station to make the short walks to 'The Weighver's Seaport', as the Lake became known. Davenport's 'Guide to Hollingworth Lake' (established in 1860) gives a glowing account of what visitors might expect as they arrived at Littleborough Station:

'turn you face towards Manchester as you alight from the train, and cross the canal on your left. A road of easy ascent, by 'Clegg's Wood', on your left, in about ten minutes brings you to the shores of Hollingworth Lake. You see nothing on your approach to indicate the existence of such a place; but keep the flagstaff in sight, and if you have any doubts about being in the right direction, you may take that for your guide. As you step on the embankment, which is considerable, and scarcely looks artificial, the broad expanse of water at once presents itself to your vision. Your first feeling on beholding it is that of astonishment that so vast a basin, lying in that cup of hills, should not have become known to you before.'

Scarcely pausing for breath and with a fine turn of Victorian enthusiasm our Guide extols the virtues of the Lake:

You are out of your everyday world - transported suddenly from regions of smoke and dust, and the sound of busy life, to where Nature herself appears to be making holiday. You will see Blackstone Edge to the east, towering above its fellows, and preaching from its rocky pulpit sermons to the solitude around; the lone 'White House', nestling in the dip of the moor, and the grey band of road winding up to the breast, until it is lost on the summit. If it be an holiday, and the

weather fine, woe to you if you come to enjoy an hour's solitude, for the lake is teeming with life. Shooting towards every point, as if they were engaged in performing an aquatic reel, an apparently countless number of boats are plying. Oars are flashing in the sun, and white sails are fluttering and gliding about as if they took as natural to fresh water as salt. The ferry steamer is churning its direct course backwards and forwards betwixt the landing stage and the pleasure gardens on the other side of the water. With very brief intervals you see it dividing the array of smaller craft, which sheer out of its way from wholesome fear of being stove in, or caught in its swell. For the fee of a penny you may take a passage on board and make acquaintance with what we once heard facetiously termed 'Th' Cheshire Side'. Probably you are like other excursionists, who immediately they leave home fancy themselves in need of refreshments: so if you feel concerned about the 'inner man', you may get a cup of coffee or tea and a 'real Eccles cake' at one of the numerous places which crowd the vicinity of the landing stage.'

But more of refreshments later; for the moment let us look at our Victorian visitor taking to the water - choice there was in plenty, and rules to be obeyed. Here are reproduced the Lake Regulations of 1872 - which will tell us that the pleasures of sailing could be had for 4d an hour, or 5s per day, but that persistently standing up in your boat meant a calling in and banishment - for that day anyway. The Pleasure Grounds on the far side were to be reached by ferry steamer and any trespasser who would not pay up was to be fined 40s (difficult to imagine when you realise this was about two week's wages in those days!) Fishing was allowed at 6d per day, or 10s per season, but woe betide those without a ticket - they were to suffer the loss of their rod and line, according to law, while shooting was not allowed at all.

Before the Lake was built there were only two hotels in the locality. **The Fisherman's Inn** on the approach from Littleborough was old established and today we can still see how this modern hostelry developed out of a group of farm buildings. The Fisherman's like many old inns has changed in recent years and carries on a brisk trade in food, drink and entertainment in comfortable surroundings - no more the sanded stone floors and wooden benches of yesteryear. The other old inn was **The Blue Ball** at Smithy Bridge - in those days a lonely retreat on the journey up to Hollingworth. The original building was demolished in recent years and on the same spot there now stands a modern hotel which extends a welcome to locals and visitors from far and wide.

With the increasing popularity of the Lake, Henry Newall and his partners wished to provide high-class refreshments at the lakeside itself - for the visitors on summer days could now be numbered in thousands - and so two new hotels were constructed. **The Beach Hotel** was a most excellent affair as can be seen from the advertisement dated 1872 and reproduced here.

below
The Old Blue Ball on Smithybridge Road, now replaced with a modern hostelry
opposite/above
The original 'Beach Hotel' shown here about 1890 and before the disastrous fire of 22 April 1901. Note the dancing stage entrance on the left
opposite/below
The Beach Hotel, rebuilt and extended after the fire, looking much the same as today

Accomodation was provided for the holidaymaker; visitors too could enjoy the refreshment rooms, while outside there were platforms for the use of picnic parties and - it was said - dancing for two thousand people, which at dusk was illuminated by gaslight. Rustic sports were on hand and - according to Davenport - 'refreshments were of the first character'. Today this hotel is still a focal point of the Lake, continuing the traditions of dining and drinking in a friendly atmostphere - though with modernisation many of the Victorian extras have now gone.

The other new venture was The **Lake Hotel and Pleasure Grounds** which were developed on the opposite side of the water where the new refreshment room now stands. The Lake Hotel was reached onfoot or by carriage around the eastern shore; or more grandly there was a steamer to ferry visitors across the Lake. Today we can still see a few remains of the old foundations of the Lake Hotel while the masses of rhododendrons and curving paths give some idea of the Pleasure Gardens as they existed a hundred years ago. The buildings, long since demolished, were described as being in the Swiss style; standing on the slope of the gardens with the floating landing-stage in front. The efficiency of the passenger steamer was guaranteed by that most excellent invention - 'The Subaqueous Telegraph - a cable laid at the bottom of the Lake whereby instant communication is held with the Booking Office and the Lake Hotel, when the ferry steamers are required on either side of the Lake'. At the rear of the buildings were a bowling green and croquet lawn bordered by the Pleasure Gardens which offered refreshments, not to mention the further delights of shrubberies and rustic arbours - all laid out by Mr Henderson of Birkenhead. In the 1860's, the proprietor George Yarwood was advertising 'Wedding Breakfasts Provided, and Pic-nic Parties liberally treated with.' On the water's edge stood a little building of charm and character. This was first built for the Rowing Club of 1860 but was later converted as refreshment rooms for the Lake Hotel. Here our Victorian tripper could take tea or enjoy a game of billiards on one of the two tables on the upper floor. Here too from the spacious balcony the visitor of a century ago could 'obtain a splendid and uninterrupted sight of any contest that may take place on the lake'. Davenport further describes the benefits of gas-lighting and the two clocks so situated that 'the visitor can easily ascertain the time to catch ferries which ran so as to meet every train that passes.' A feature I have read about was a statue in stone and clay moulding, supposed to represent a shipwrecked sailor on the look-out. It was made by Charles Prescot of Smithy Bridge and presented to Henry Newall who placed it here at the Lake - I have never been able to discover what happened to the statue.

These two hotels were by no means enough to meet the demand - easy to imagine when you learn that 6,000 miners met at the Lake for a conference on 13 August 1866; so more hotels and refreshment rooms grew up. It is said that most private houses in the vicinity had notices in their windows offering 'Tea in Jugs and Sandwiches served' or 'Hot Water Cheap'. There were, at this time, about eight well advertised unlicensed refreshment rooms round the Lake; the best known being Alfred Mills at **Good Templar House** in Smithy Bridge and W Butterworth's **Temperance Hall** - sometimes known as **Yorkshire House**. Hotels and houses were also advertising 'Liberal allowances for school parties' and 'Good Stabling' as well as 'Cigarettes, Cigars and Wines'. Business was booming.

Of the other main hotels **The Mermaid**, now no more, had on its wall a stone dated 1777 but experts think that this, without any letters and in an amateur style, was of doubtful standing. The Mermaid stood on the way up to Hollingworth Fold and was very popular; not least during the middle of the last century when it was tenanted by Mr Sladen who was already involved in business at the Lake. Later proprietors in the 60's and 70's were Henry Taylor and George Travis. The Mermaid finally closed its doors in 1911.

opposite/above
The Lake Hotel described as being in the 'Swiss' style; the photographs were probably taken around 1900. The fine sun canopy carries the name 'Sladens'. In 1896 the Rochdale Canal Co had leased the Lake Hotel and various pieces of land to Uriah Sladen for a rent of £150 yearly. This included the exclusive rights to let out boats for hire and operate the steamers, plus the fishing rights
opposite/below
The 'Lodge Inn' on the road to Rakewood. This photograph dates from about 1900; the sign carries the name Benjiman Chadwick and advertises Foreign and British Spirits, Ale, Porter and Tobacco. The Lodge Inn is now converted into two houses

The **Lodge Inn** opened in 1826 and provided welcome refreshment at Rakewood for many years. From advertisements we can see that the landlord in 1865 was Mr Solomon Butterworth who was followed some years later by Mr R Slinger. Both gentlemen appear to have been enthusiastic hosts and as well as accomodation for holidaymakers they were offering 'Dinners, Chops, Steaks, Tea, Coffee etc - and good stabling'. It is interesting to note that 'Good Stabling' was a claim made by all the hotels in the district and the comfort of the horse was obviously of great importance in this period - some fifty years before the arrival of the motor car. The Lodge Inn finally closed in 1917 and is now converted into two modern houses.

On the south side of the Lake, between the Beach and the Lake Hotel, a wellknown farm at Peanock which had a date of 1770 but was mentioned as being owned by the Belfields in a deed of 1600, was rebuilt in 1857 as **The Queens Hotel.** An early landlord was Charles Buckley who proclaimed 'visitors to this Fashionable Place of Resort can be supplied with Foreign and British Spirits, Wines, Ales, Etc' while somewhat later in 1872 this hotel was advertised as **Marlands, Queens Hotel** - Ten Minutes Walk from Smithy Bridge Station - with A Spacious Pavilion and Dancing Stage in the Grounds adjoining the Hotel'. This was available for picnics, wedding parties, schools and clubs and capable of dining 200 persons. The Queens also offered 'Apartments with Attendance' and of course 'Good Stabling'. Today this is no longer a Licenced hotel and the buildings have reverted back to something like their original use as a farm dwelling.

The demand for accommodation and refreshment was still not fulfilled and in 1876 a large new hotel was built on Lake Bank opposite the landing stage. This was the **Lancashire and Yorkshire Hotel;** commanding an impressive view over the Lake and offering every accommodation together with an outdoor dancing platform of 18,360 square feet and a band in attendance daily. This central hotel effectively catered for the increased business at the Lake but, like the Lake Hotel, it was later demolished and in its place today is a small group of fine houses which were built using the stone from the hotel.

There was also the **Star Inn**, close to the Fishermans, now a private house, and which got its name from the hill behind it, known as Cleggswood Stars. Finally at each station, Littleborough and Smithy Bridge, there were hotels, both suitably named

Railway. The one at Smithy Bridge closed some years ago and has since had various uses but the **Railway Hotel**, Littleborough is still a very busy and popular inn today. Also at Three Lane Ends, Smithy Bridge stood a small Beer House - **The Royal Oak**, now demolished, and noted for the form outside where local pensioners still sit and put the world to rights.

opposite/above
The Lancashire and Yorkshire Hotel, long since demolished, which stood on Lakebank and was the last of the hotels to be built at the Lake. The stone from this building was used to construct the houses which now stand on the same site. Dancing was a major attraction during late Victorian times - there appears to have been indoor and outdoor dancing. The large circular fittings were probably gas or carbon type lamps to provide illumination at night
opposite/below
Rakewood in 1917, showing open fields where the new sports ground now stands. On the far left are the houses at Antioch

Work, as well as play

As well as being a resort for pleasure the district carried on its day to day work as it had always done. It is beyond the scope of this book to look closely at the development of farming and industry, but, a few notes will help to show that this was indeed an area which provided a variety of livings and employment. Farming was carried on mainly in small units concerned with dairy cattle and sheep grazing with the largest being the old established settlement of Whittaker which still looks down on the Lake today - although there farming has partly given way to golf - very much a fresh-air sport, set as it is at the edge of the Moor. The sheep needed to be hardy too, with Lonks and Grit stones being the main breeds, which were nearly wild.

Today farming is still carried on and plays an important role in the life of the district; though some of the outlying farms are in ruins while others have been bought and turned into country homes.

Rakewood has long been a small centre of industry. Holroyd's were going at Rakewood Mill for nearly fifty years and were themselves successors to Halliwells who were recorded as being textile waste dealers in 1872. Holroyd's became part of a West Yorkshire Group and the Mill has lately been used for processing flour and similar substances. Cleggs have been at Rakewood for four generations and are still active as textile finishers - originally in woollens and blankets but of late with modern textiles and man made fibres. At the same firm finished cloth is also made up into completed articles. Perhaps the most interesting of the works was Wilson's Tannery at Booth Hollins, which made good use of the clear moorland water. A disastrous fire about fifty years ago stopped the tannery and Wilsons abandoned Booth Hollins in favour of their larger factory at Wigan. The buildings still standing are used by a local farmer for storing farm machinery.

In the last 30 years or so a new industry has developed which is now one of the main employers in the area. This is the Akzo Chemie (UK) Ltd - (Armour-Hess) - chemical works alongside the canal on the way up to the Lake from Littleborough Station - covering several acres this is an extensive complex of machinery and steel towers; something of a monument to modern industrial times, working round the clock and at night being illuminated by bright points of light which appear to hang high in the sky.

opposite
A drawing of the mills at Rakewood 1850
below
View over Armour Hess (Akzo Chemie) towards Littleborough about 1950

Coal pits and quarries

The tinkle of a bell and the patter of hooves on stones told of the approach of a string of 'Galloways' with their paniers full and steadily making their way down the Rakewood Valley towards Tunshill Colliery and Rochdale. The packhorse and the little ponies, donkeys or mules were the common means of transport over the rough, very poor moorland pathways or tracks and were a feature of the district until near the end of the 19th Century. Probably the last of these was 'Ailse o' Fussers' (Alice Hartley) and her string of donkeys, often muzzled for speed and bringing lime and limestone from East Lancashire over Reddyshore, Wardle and to Whitworth. Sometimes also could be seen a cart drawn by mule or pony and followed by a man, wife and children all with 'lading cans' and a load of sandstone to be sold at houses 'Penorth or apporth' a time, to scour the stone flagged domestic kitchens. These would be the Smallbridge Sandknockers or Kitter Street lads as they were called.

The moors and hills around Hollingworth Lake were riddled with small coal pits and quarries and wells and some coal pits were quite large as at Ealees, Whittaker and Tunshill with its tramway; as also Schofield Hall pit which had coke ovens, also Smithy Bridge, Rakewood Holme Pit and Dearnley. Many local coal mines were 'brest hi' - not deep pits with shafts as we know them today but cut into the sloping ground and down. Two such firms were James Lees of 'Hollingworth Colliery and Coke Burners' at Syke and J Taylor and Co of 'Whittaker Colliery' at Ealees. All mineral rights belonged to the absentee Lord of the Manor, Baron Byron of Newstead whose agent Simon Dearden, Solicitor of Handle Hall Littleborough and The Orchard, Rochdale collected royalties, took his commission and sent the rest to the Lord of the Manor who was never satisfied. Law suits took place in late 18th and early 19th Centuries and when Lord George Gordon succeeded he at first continued but later in 1823 sold out to Dearden, who assumed the title and changed his Rochdale home to 'The Manor House' whilst Byron went to enjoy himself in Venice and died later gaining fame as a supporter of Greek Independence at Missolonghi in 1828.

The pits and quarries gradually closed as the new owner was as avaricious as Byron but the Coal Strike of 1926 saw many re-opened and evidence can still be seen of these workings. Perhaps the two most interesting of the coal pits were Cleggswood and the Holme Pit. This latter was full of water and a pumping station in Halliday Lane pumped the overflow onto the railway lines at Clegg Hall where it went into troughs and the express LMS trains scooped it up to refill their tanks when travelling at speed. This operation was mechanically controlled by a device put in by Mr L Holden in the 1930's.

The Cleggswood pit, near Inghams Lane and the Littleboro Railway Hotel, had a tramway down the hill and through the space between the terraced houses, across the road and then down to barges on the canal. This like many local pits was owned and worked by Knowles of Wigan.

In Smithybridge was a brickworks once owned by Walmersleys and later by Hall and Rogers who manufactured not only bricks, but chimney tops, fire bricks and sanitary tubes (drain pipes presumably). This area became known as 'The Pottery Yard' and is now built over with Council houses and garages. Business life also included small shops, selling food and essential provisions and those I will mention here were James Butterworth of Hollingworth Fold, James Leach of Lower Abbots Knowl, James Gooder and Charles Crossley both at Lake Bank and Horrocks Clegg and Co of Rakewood.

The latter half of the nineteenth centry saw the Lake at the height of its popularity and entertainment and sport prospered. The Rowing Club which had started in 1860 folded up and its assets were taken over by the Lake developers but it started again in 1872 and has never looked back. This club has seen rapid growth in the last 30 years, has enjoyed success in competitions and now has a modern club house with up-to-date facilities. Fishing also developed as a sport and owing to the absence of natural local fish the Lake has been stocked with fish on various occasions - notably 30,000 bream, dace and perch were introduced in 1863, and I believe that trout were put in not many years ago. I shall return to the sporting scene again, so for a moment let us take a glance at the entertainments which tempted and amused the visitors a century ago.

Along Lake Bank, particularly by the steamer landing stage, there rapidly grew up a variety of stalls and small lock-up shops selling souvenirs, gifts, sweets and snacks. On special holidays, just as today, the Lake attracted more visitors and this brought in the fortune teller, cheapjacks, conjurers and tricksters as well as the Gypsies who would camp in the Ealess Valley - and all trying to make money out of the not so simple Lancashire working man. Today we still have the visiting fair on Bank Holidays. Photography, still in its early days, seems to have held a fascination for the holiday-maker. This was in the days when cameras

The landing stage of the Lake Hotel side in 1884, showing the steamer, 'Neptune'. The Lancashire and Yorkshire Hotel with its outdoor dancing platforms can be seen on the far right

were the domain of the professional photographer - using his glass plates before modern films appeared - and a photograph would be a treasured memento of a day out, and a way for the working man to obtain family portraits; something he could never afford before the invention of the camera. From Davenport's Guide we can get some idea of popular photography at the lake. At the Pleasure Grounds were James Milton and later a Mr Whitham, both offering a high-class service; Mr Milton being at pains to explain that good portraits could be obtained without bright sunshine while Mr Whitham offered portraits on glass or paper plus a 'Variety of Local Views including instantaneous views of cloud and wave'. On the Lake Bank side were Robinson's Photographic Rooms and Kenworthy's Photographic Gallery; which also included Kenworthy's Bazaar selling 'Fancy Goods suitable for Presents'. Near Mr Sladen's Hotel (The Beach) was Mr Garside's Photographic Establishment and around by the Fisherman's Inn Mr Lancaster advised you to bring your relatives or friends to be photographed - especially, he intimated, as one day they would die or perhaps emigrate! Other delights included a Camera

Obscura and a Stereoscopic Exhibition, both near the landing stage; while at the Beach Hotel was advertised a 'Gymnasium'.

What local person, of the right age of course, can ever forget the pleasure of a ride on the famous 'Bobby Horses'. This was a roundabout situated near the landing stage - all colours with flashing manes and tails going round and round to music. This fairground ride was probably built around 1860 for about that time the owner, Mr Sucksmith, advertised it as his 'Steam

below
Lakebank in 1908. The shop and the public hall both carry the name H Nichol
opposite/above
An artist's illustration of the Lake Hotel Pleasure Grounds 1880. The hotel is on the far right. The nearer building is the refreshment room where the balcony was a favourite viewpoint for events on the Lake
opposite/below
Hollingworth Lake by moonlight; an artists drawing of 1880. The steamer, seen here on the Lake Hotel side, ran a regular service for passengers across the Lake

LAKE BANK HOLLINGWORTH

Horses - wooden horses 6 feet high, the largest of the kind ever made, propelled by steam power, which are quite safe and easy to ride'. The Bobby Horses remained at the Lake until after the last war continuing to be the wonderment and joy of children who thought these large beautiful animals with their flowing manes and swishing tails were real and alive. When, as often happened, pieces were broken; ears, legs and the like breaking away, then Mills the Joiners, of Smithy Bridge repaired or replaced them. Mr Sam Gould who ran them for many years saw the power change from hand-winch to steam, and gas, and finally to electricity. Bought by Mr Mann, well-known for his interest in Amusement and Fairground activities, they later went to New Brighton and finally, the horses only, went to the USA. They were much missed and are still often spoken about for the simple pleasure they gave to so many.

A noted local writer on the Rochdale area was William Robertson. Here, from his 'Guide to Rochdale' is how he saw the Lake in the year 1875:

'So, though Hollingworth is neither a Derwentwater nor a Killarney, it may and does possess attractions of a special nature worth viewing. It is homely; it is pleasant; and it is the lake of South Lancashire and the Riding; the charming spot where on gala days gather thousands of workers in this teeming district. Leeds sends excursions; Manchester makes holiday here; contingents flock from Bradford, and Bury, and Oldham; and not a district among the moors but is proud if its amateur instrumentalists can score well at a Hollingworth brass band contest. On a summer afternoon there is a wonderful natural variety at Hollingworth. Its elevated position unfolds a wide panorama. Over the sombre hued Blackstone Edge and russet tinged moorland of Wardle, light and shade play strange antics. The heather on Whittaker moor is bathed in colours an artist would give his eyes to catch, while, to the south-west, over the murky atmospheric tinge which tells where Rochdale is, the champaign country rolls towards Manchester in undulating waves of meadowland, absorbing the brilliant sunshine and throwing back hues attuned in harmony with the amphitheatre of surrounding hills. Upon the Lake itself, float or dart craft of every description - the racing skiff, the pleasure boat, the fishing punt, and the snorting ferry steamer - glide in every direction, leaving in their wakes long lines of glittering sheen, while on the western bank linger crowds for whose patronage numerous caterers of sweets, and toys, and tea, clamour in no uncertain voice. For those of more robust appetite, the many hotels which fringe the lake offer every accomodation'.

And so Robertson put into words the great changes which had occurred since 1800 when a simple lodge was built to supply water for the Canal and we can see how the Lake justified its reputation as 'The Weighver's Seaport'.

Hollingworth Lake and District as shown on the Ordnance Survey Map of 1889-91. Most of the old buildings and places shown are still recognisable today. There is little building around the Lake itself; between Smithybridge and the Beach Hotel lies a country road with open fields all around. This land is now built up with housing to an extent which could hardly have been envisaged in those days. Of the many inns shown, only the 'Beach' and the 'Fisherman's' remain around the Lake itself; the Armour Hess area is shown as 'Cloughfield Works'. The map shows the three embankments built to hold back the water to form a lake - [1] at Hollingworth Bank [2] between the 'Lancashire and Yorkshire Hotel' and the 'Fisherman's' and [3] on the south side near the Boat House. Map loaned by Rochdale Library and reproduced by courtesy of the Ordnance Survey.

Before going any further into the happenings in Victorian times let us take a look at the country parts around the Lake, for they also have a story to tell.

Soon after leaving the Fishermans Inn we see on the left the slope into the Ealees Valley with footpaths leading towards Littleborough and up to Whittaker; beyond lies the rocky outline of Robin Hoods Bed - a magnificent skyline in all weathers. The Ealees Valley was at one time used by local churches and chapels for cricket and picnics and is now envisaged as a part of the Country Park; with the new Information Centre and car park built on the site of the old council tip. Proceeding along the bank towards Rakewood we first pass Hollingworth Fold, otherwise called Hollingworth Village, where there are several old stone-built dwellings including a Victorian Schoolchapel now being converted into a house and an 'Iron Church' near the site of Hollingworth Workhouse. The past is echoed in several buildings with date stones including Hollingworth Fold Cottage, which has a doorway lintel marked IMF 1727. This was sometimes called Croy Cottage - but why? Higher Fold Farm has a date of 1668 and the Shippon carries the date 1674. Further down the lane we find No 5, Syke which is dated 1755 whilst Syke Farm itself was built in 1758. Inside the main Farmhouse at Syke there is said to be a witchpost or charm engraved to ward off evil spirits.

These buildings in the fold, which go back 250 years and more hold memories of long forgotten moorland folk whose lives must often have been a long struggle. In this small area are the remains of Old Hollingworth which was a busy place in the last century with its church, two schools and a workhouse. The 'Charity' School was founded on 18 August 1726 by Richard Townley, Alexander Butterworth and others. This school received help from the Hill Family, partic-

opposite

Hollingworth Fold about 70 years ago. The large building in the centre is the Mermaid Inn. On the top right is the old workhouse

below

Photograph taken in 1890 showing the cobbled road at the bottom of Hollingworth, leading up to the Fold. The ruined building which projects behind the houses on the top left is the old pump house where a steam engine was used to raise water from the Lake up to the level of the Drain, where it then flowed about 4 miles round the hills to the Canal at Summit

ularly from the will of John Hill in 1727 in which he left annual amounts to the school and also to Ogden School up above Rakewood. The village school with its one teacher did excellent work and the Saddleworth author Ammon Wrigley in his account of the 'Moorland School' and its lonely woman teacher paints a vivid word picture of such schools. There was also at Hollingworth, a Dame's School where an alphabet was carved on a large stone. This 'Alphabet Stone' was commented on by Ammon Wrigley who said it was at the old 'Mermaid Inn' on one of his visits, before it closed in 1911. Later, when Mr Harry Percival of Fair View, who was an authority on Hollingworth affairs, went to find the stone it had gone. Mr Percival traced the owner but neither he nor Mr Stott of Rochdale Museum could persuade him to sell the alphabet stone or lend it for public view. However, when in the 1950's the Littleborough Council did some work in the area, it was said that the alphabet stone and a fine stone porch were removed to Harehill Park; but I am not aware that they are still in the locality today. The story of this stone is based on the old Dame's School in the Fold. While

she was busy with domestic affairs, as well as teaching basic letters, her pupils destroyed their alphabet papers; so a local mason said 'I'll cure 'em' and carved the alphabet in capitals and small letters on a stone over the fireplace. (These two schools are now no more, numbers not individuals counting more these days). James Royds, who was master at Hollingworth School in mid-Victorian times, wrote a small book telling a story based on the area and called *'Abbots Knowl - A Lancashire Legend'* published by that short lived paper *The Rochdale Pilot* in 1858.

At Hollingworth Fold the prominent 'Iron Church' of St Hilda's Mission, C of E is of interest for it was previously at Featherstall, Littleborough serving St Mary's RC Parish. The building, made of metal sheets, was sold to Hollingworth through the Mother Church at Milnrow, out of the Hill Charity, and was re-erected here with structural modifications in 1931 and is now divided as a meeting room and church; much of the work being done by a small but keen group of local people. The St Hilda patronage was suggested by Canon Raines for the previous schoolchapel as he was born at Whitby where his grandfather was Vicar of St Hilda's, the church on the hill; and so it was an appropriate name for the church on the hill at Hollingworth.

The old workhouse at Hollingworth Fold was one of a group set up in 1837 when the Rochdale Union was started, but there had been a workhouse here for years before. Harry Percival had a collection of old papers on the locality which included rate papers for this area (Butterworth) showing that in May 1785 the workhouse rates were 12s 6½d; whilst Canon Raines speaks of a metal date plate showing 1707IH, the initials of the Hill family. The rate for the nearby Schofield Hall was £8 4s 3d; a measure of its importance. It was stated that this workhouse catered for about 60 inmates; men, women and children who attended Hollingworth School. Hooks and fastenings in the walls were said to be for chaining or fastening up difficult inmates. In 1868 there was an official inspection of the Union work-

The old workhouse at Hollingworth Fold, set behind a fine stone wall with an iron gate. The workhouse closed down a hundred years ago with the opening of the new workhouse at Dearnley, now Birch Hill Hospital. The workhouse was demolished around 1940

houses in Marland, Spotland, Wardleworth and Hollingworth. The inspector's report included the following comments on the Hollingworth Workhouse:

'This old and ill-constructed building does not afford the accomodation and arrangements to be found in every proper workhouse establishment. It contains 44 men, 12 women and 3 children; 59 inmates in all at the present time, 15 of these are imbeciles or idiotic persons. The men for the most part sleep together two in the same bed, an indecent and unwholesome practice which cannot too speedily be put an end to. There is no paid nurse and the male pauper in charge of medicine for the men cannot read writing. He cannot therefore be trusted with the duty of giving medicine, etc. To show how little discipline or control is kept up here, calling at the neighbouring public house I found pauper inmates of the workhouse in the taproom, etc.

However, changes were made in the workhouse system in Rochdale following Alderman Livesey's struggle with the Ministry in London and as a result a large Union workhouse was built at Dearnley in 1879; which we know today as Birch Hill Hospital; and so the smaller workhouses were closed. Several of the Hollingworth Workhouse Masters have their names recorded; the last was James Hey with his wife as matron.

There are several old buildings and remains around the Lake but none so important or well recorded as Schofield Hall, the home of the Schofields as far back as 1310. This building was described by Canon Raines MA FSA, Vicar of Milnrow in his revision of Notita Cestrensis in 1849 as 'a large handsome house in the Elizabethan style but in a remote part of his parish'. Here, in the 15th year of Edward II, lived John de Scholfeld who had many disputes with the Abbot of Whalley over land; Rochdale being indirectly in the Parish of the Abbey of Whalley. A full pedigree of this family can be found in Fishwick's 'History of the Parish of Rochdale'. Coming down to Captain James Scholfeld in 1664 we find the family in poor circumstances, his estate having suffered much from his loyalty to the King in the Civil War, and in 1673 he sold the Hall to his son-in-law, Seth Clayton. By 1770 the family was dispersed and Schofield Hall had been sold to Robert Entwistle of Foxholes, Rochdale and again later it was sold or let in separate lots. The last of the Schofield's was the Rev Radcliffe Scholefield who was for many years rector of the Old Meeting Home in Birmingham where he lived with his sister, Josepha. He died in 1803 and as they were both unmarried the long line of Schofields came to an end. There are many people in this district with the name Schofield but none, I think, are directly connected with the old family at Schofield Hall; although as recently as 1975 a gentleman, long resident in France, was enquiring if his ancestors were connected with this ancient family. It is interesting to see from records that the spelling of the name often varies.

Schofield Hall was in fairly good condition before the 1914-18 War when it was due to be sold for export - to be taken down and rebuilt in the United States of America. However, the war prevented this and the building was left to crumble away at the mercy of the rough moorland weather, leaving a few remains and over six hundred years of memories. An incident connected with the Hall occurred in the late 16th century when Cuthbert Scholfield came riding home from Rochdale Market to find his wife with one Michael Goodricke, a gentleman. The surprised couple made their escape through a window, hotly pursued by the husband violently waving his sword. As Ann was the daughter of the Lord of the Manor, Lord Byron of Newstead, she was able to obtain a divorce and if anything it was Cuthbert's character which suffered as a result.

There are other interesting old Farmsteads and Houses in the Lake area and apart from those which are right out on the moors and now derelict the others remain and are still run mainly as farms or, in some cases, as private residences. Many of these farms are mentioned in Fishwick's book and have histories going back over three or four hundred years. They include Wild House, Birchinley, Bib Knowl ('Bible Knoll'), Turnough, Low House, Brearley, Sheep Bank and Whittaker.

Fishwick records that Whittaker, which stands on the slope above the Ealees Valley, was known as Quitacres in the 13th century and afterwards was variously called Whitacres and White Acre. In 1336 the land appears to have been owned by William de Whitacres but from at least 1461 and thereafter for about 400 years it was held by the Schofield Family; although from about 1600 they began to sell off portions of the land including 'Bryerlye', now called Brearley Farm in 1614 and a year later the lands at Lanefoot and Oken Holt (Owlet Hall) were transferred by Abraham Schofield to his brother Jacob. Sheepbank Farm was also part of Whittaker and was lived in by generations of Schofields. What is now the Golf Club

Schofield Hall in 1803

was sold to James Travis of Walsden in 1650; there are date stones of IT MT 1669 and IT MT 1724, the latter at Sheepbank, (T stands for Travis). A later James Travis sold out to Thomas Lord of Calliards, Dearnley in 1802. Samuel Lord and Edmund Turner, also of Calliards, rebuild most of the buildings in 1850, (having already rebuilt Brierley Farm in 1829); placing a datestone - Rebuilt ETS Lord 1850 - on the buildings. Not far from the Lake, on the Rochdale side, is the famous Clegg Hall recorded in history and Lancashire legends; not least for its 'Boggart'. Roby and the Rev Oakley both

Views of Schofield Hall, from 1803; around 1900 and the ruins of more recent years

tell variants of this ghost story but I very much doubt the existence of a tunnel from Clegg Hall to Stubley Hall. The names of Clegg and Belfield are recorded here in the 13th and 16th centuries but it was probably an Assheton who built the present Hall around 1620; which replaced another building which had stood for 200 years - which itself was said to be a continuation of another hall of 1135 AD. In the first half of the last century Clegg Hall was used as a licensed public house known as 'The Black Sloven', after a hunter belonging to the Fenton Family who then owned the Hall. It is now empty and in recent years was suggested as a Folk Museum but nothing came of Councillor Sam Howard's efforts.

The Lake has always been popular with folk round-about and none loved it more than a local gentleman, Arnold Schofield of Stubley Hall, who was somewhat eccentric. On a fine day he would say to his man-servant: 'Patrick, I think we will go fishing (or shooting according to the mood). Get the trap and other things ready'. Off they would drive in the pony trap to the landing stage at the Lake to take out his private boat, lock up and row across to the Rakewood end. 'It's a lovely afternoon, let us rest awhile and see what cook has put up'. After the food and beer had been enjoyed he would invariably say 'Well, time for a nap', and so anchored they would take a long rest in the sunshine; upon waking Arnold would say 'Just time to row back to be home for the evening meal'; and so the pair returned from their sporting afternoon. He also rode a penny-farthing bicycle and was often seen riding up to and right round the Lake in his sporting 'Norfolk' suit.

Other locals were noted for regular early morning swimming until it became almost a joke - 'Where have you been?' - 'Just keeping fit, swam twice across'. A daring feat occurred on 22 January 1879 when one man drove his horse and trap right across the ice on the frozen lake and arrived safely on the other side. I was told recently by a well-known Hollingworth man that returning from Rochdale with his father during one hard winter they paused to consider how long it would take to walk round in the difficult conditions. They were joined by Mr Jackson, the Waterman and the third generation of his family to hold that office, who said 'Don't waste your time struggling round - walk across', and big man that he was he set off from the Beach Hotel across the ice which creaked and groaned. 'If it will carry him, it will take us' they concluded and so they followed in the dark until all three got across safe and sound. Many will remember Mr Jackson's daughter who died recently aged 90, having lived in the Waterman's Cottage in Hollingworth Fold all her life.

Going towards Rakewood, on the left past the old Lodge Inn, lies a small area known as 'Antioch', named after the old Methodist Chapel. Behind here is Abbots Knowl and further back, according to old maps were the coal pits and coke ovens of Schofield Hall Colliery.

Clegg Hall in1831. From an engraving by Finden

Rakewood itself is still very much alive with industry and sport; Cleggs still busy after four generations; a new industry at Holroyds and modernisation of the houses; as well as very progressive development of the Rochdalians Club with so many varying activities for young people. The area is now overlooked by the fine M62 viaduct, the modern route for goods across the Pennines - making a journey which once took days over moorland tracks into one of a few hours on the wide new Motorway.

Just approaching the Lake Hotel site we see to the left, a modern, well-kept caravan site, part of which is permanent and the rest for tourists and which does not unduly affect the country aspect. There are many farms and buildings about. Some, such as Bib Knowl, Wild House, Turnough, Shaw Moss, Low House have been modernised and yet remain in character with the local scene.

In order to gain an idea of how people in the Lake area lived and worked over a hundred years ago, we can look at the old Ordnance Survey Maps. It is surprising to see, that even after the coming of the canal and railway, there were few areas of buildings as we know them today. Apart from the old farms and inns already mentioned there were a few cottages and little else. Nearly all the land was farmed; Hollingworth Village was the main settlement and before the Beach Hotel was built there appear to have been no buildings at all from Three Lane Ends right round to the Fisherman's Inn. What are now called Smithybridge Road and Lake Bank were known as 'Fens Lane'. The site of the present Rowing and Sailing Clubs was 'Black Butts' while the Lake Hotel on the far side was to be built on land called 'Black's Nursery'. The old maps show that apart from farming and woollen and cotton mills at Rakewood the main work was in coal pits and quarries.

There is reference to a gasometer at Rakewood which must have been associated with nearby coal pits and coke ovens.

At that time, old roads in the area, were much as they are today, although of course they would be narrower and not always made up. An important route seems to have been Cleggs Wood Lane which ran from near the site of the Lancashire and Yorkshire Hotel down to the canal bridge next to the present Armour Hess works. This had a link across to Three Lane Ends through what is now the new private housing estate. The old maps show Hollingworth Road from Littleborough up to the Fishermans as being 'Private' in part, this was perhaps associated with the Canal Company at that time.

In the last century the Lake was also an attraction for so-called sportsmen whose hobby was shooting every strange bird they saw. It is recorded for example:

'On 6 May 1865 a fine specimen of the black-necked speckled sea diver (probably a large black backed diver) strayed from its usual course to the Northern climes and was shot by a keen eyed sportsman making a valuable addition to his collection'.

I am glad to say that with the modern approach to the study of wild life these rare visitors are noted with interest and allowed to pass on their way unharmed, rather than becoming an exhibit in someone's glass case. There are rare species on and around the Lake area and these are well written about in the local papers by men like Messrs Marshall and Soothill. Referring to the variety of wild life in the Guide of 1872 Davenport says 'with all these activities and interests Hollingworth may be fairly called a People's Park in the future' - and that just over a century later, is what will become the Hollingworth Lake Country Park.

Lake View Children's Hospital

Not far along the road to Wild House and Milnrow are some recently built houses, behind an attractive red brick wall. This is the site of the former Lake View Children's Hospital which was demolished a few years ago. The onset of infectious diseases in Victorian times and in the early years of this 20th Century caused many problems and varied treatment was given. Children with Scarlet Fever, Dyptheria and similar contagious illnesses were removed to moorland cottages and isolated. About seventy years ago the Rochdale Hospital Committee built this children's hospital on the hill overlooking the Lake for such a purpose and it served well, although the term 'Bleaked Hill' caused many to feel dismayed. There have been no reported cases of Dyptheria or Scarlet Fever for some years now and today most other children's illnesses can be treated in other ways, so the Isolation Hospital became redundant. After much renovation it became known as the 'Lake View Children's Home' and was used for convalescent children and special cases. The children enjoyed the fresh air and country atmostphere and were able to sample the pleasures of the Lake. The place was closed around 1960 and offered for sale and at one time the Salford Rescue Society thought of using it, but here again the move away from institutional life to home training ended the idea. The whole place was pulled down and sold and private houses have been built on the site in the last few years.

This was the title given by Press and Public to Mr Thomas Stott (1842-1914) of Littleborough who was the boatman at the Lake in Victorian times, and who during his many years of service, was reputed to have saved the lives of nearly 40 people. He was employed as a boatman at the Lake over 80 years ago and spent his time with the sailing boats and rowing boats which were very popular. Unfortunately those who hired these craft had little knowledge of handling them and no experience of the varying moods of the Lake itself. Mr Stott, though no swimmer himself had own methods of rescue, and was modest, speaking little of this efforts. He never received monetary reward but had many momentos given him and was very proud of an illuminated address, subscribed for and given to him by his admirers as a 'token of his unselfish service'. This, with newspaper cuttings and a poem, have been preserved by his descendants. The poem, part of which I have here, was written by Roger Standring; Boot and Shoe dealer in Yorkshire Street, Rochdale, who also published a book of poems all about deeds of bravery and which was much admired by his Baillie Street Methodist friends. Mr Stott, on one occasion, was nearly drowned in rescuing three people whose boat had overturned. All came out of the Lake safely.

He retired from the Lake as boatman when trade died down and afterwards worked for a local contractor. He died in 1914 and was buried at the Littleborough Parish Church by Rev AC McIntyre with some degree of honour. He left three sons, Jack Stott, Joe Stott a great church worker, Robert who lived in Burnley, and a daughter - who became Mrs Brierley. Her daughter Mrs Ingham has given me most of this information and the right to publish this poem, which I have edited slightly. It is an interesting tale, though the literary merit does not quite match the talents of the Hero.

The Hollingworth Hero
by R Standring, Rochdale

Who would not like to see
The HERO of the Lake
Who to save his fellowmen
Twenty time placed dear life at stake

One brilliant summer's day
Tom was working at the Lake
When far distant from the shore
He heard a plaintive shriek

Bounding o'er a bank
He Sprang into a boat
Seized oars with skilful hands
And turned the boat about

Soon he was alongside
The inverted boat he steered
Where human forms were struggling
Whose shrieks he had heard on shore

Hurrying to the rescue
Ere long all were safe
The HERO wise and brave
Had saved them from a watery grave

Tho' not a farthing Tom was given
Not a thank you by anyone he saved
Yet almost from the jaws of death
He had risked life and breath

We think the quenchless fire
Of the gallant hero's love
Must surely have been kindled
By the hand that rules above

opposite
The Hollingworth Hero

The Rakewood Viaduct

The Rakewood Viaduct which carries the M62 motorway from Lancashire into Yorkshire was begun in 1966 and opened to motorway traffic in October 1971. The viaduct crosses the valley with a total span of about 840 feet and is supported on twenty reinforced concrete columns which themselves carry the massive steel girders under the motorway. At either end the hillsides were cut away by giant earth moving machines to maintain the long gradient into Yorkshire where the M62 was built over some of the most difficult terrain ever encountered in road building in this country. Working through the Pennine winters on the rough moors, the motorway men were known to say the weather was so bad - 'it rained up your trouser legs.' The design and construction of the viaduct was supervised by the Lancashire County Surveyor, the contractor was Reed and Mallik Ltd.

July 1967, the columns supporting the viaduct are almost complete. Through one of the centre spans is a new open drain which also carries the water from the diverted Longden End Brook before it reaches the Lake. Beyond the viaduct is the contractor's site base, close to Rakewood itself, and further on the broad expanse of Hollingworth Lake.

January 1969 saw the main viaduct works complete and the way was open to motorway construction vehicles. It was to be another 2½ years before the motorway was finished and open to traffic. Just beyond the Lake is the old Lodge Inn and on the hill to the left is Schofield Hall Farm. At its greatest height the motorway stands 140 feet above the valley bottom.

Photographs by courtesy of the Lancashire County Surveyor

Winter at the Lake

Hollingworth is a place to be enjoyed all the year round for as winter closes in the Lake takes on quite a different appearance. On clear frosty days with snow on Blackstone Edge, the moors have a look of the Alps, and with the partly frozen water it has a beauty of its own. The Lake has been completely frozen over many times with varying depths of ice. In 1860 and again in 1864 it is on record that nearly 2,000 people skated; whilst curling matches were played between teams from Leeds, Manchester and Liverpool; and even a cricket match between two Rochdale teams was played on the ice. Again in 1871 James Schofield and the Rev W Haines organised a match on the thickly frozen lake.

Edwin Waugh, the famous Lancashire writer, who resided at Peanock in 1860 gives this vivid description of winter at the Lake, in 'Lancashire Sketches' 1867:

'In winter, the landscape about 'Hollingworth' is wild and lonesome; and the water is sometimes so completely frozen over that a horse and light vehicle may be driven across it, from bank to bank, a mile's distance. It is a favourite resort of skaters, from the surrounding districts; though the ice is often dangerously uneven in some places, by reason of strong springs, and other causes. Many accidents have happened through skating upon insecure parts in the ice of this water. Going home late one night in the depth of

opposite
Happy days on the ice in March 1947; looking towards Rakewood. The Lake has been frozen over many times and although there have been accidents and drownings, things look safe enough on this occasion; even cricket matches have been played on the ice
below
Winter at Hollingworth Lake 1912

winter, to my residence by the side of this lake, I found the midnight scene dimly illuminated in the distance by a gleam of lights upon the lake; and the sound of pick-axes breaking up the ice, fell with a startling significance upon the ear. Our dog 'Captain', did not come out to meet me, when I whistled, as usual; and I hurried, by a short cut over the fields and through the wood, towards the spot where the lights were visible. There I found a company of farmers and weavers, standing upon the bank, with one or two of the wealthy employers from the village of Littleborough, who had drags in their hands, and were giving directions to a number of workmen who were breaking a channel for the passage of a boat to the spot where the ice had broken in with the weight of three young men belonging to the neighbourhood. This melancholy midnight gathering were working by lantern-light, to recover the bodies from the water. I remained upon the spot until two of the corpses were brought to the bank, and removed in a cart to the farm-house where I resided, previous to being conveyed to their homes in the distant town, later on in the morning, and while it was yet dark. I shall never forget the appearance of those fresh-looking youths, as they lay stretched side by side, in their skating gear, upon a table, in the long passage which led up to my bed-chamber.

below
Smithybridge Road looking towards Birch Hill Hospital; the heavy snows in 1947
opposite/above
Heavy snows in February 1942 cover the railway line at Smithbridge Station. This view towards Rochdale shows the old Station buildings, now demolished. All that remain today are the level crossing gates and the signal box
opposite/below
The day after the tragic railway accident at Smithy bridge station. On the night of 18 March 1915, in bad weather, the Leeds to Fleetwood Boat Express crashed at high speed into an empty stock train on the Littleborough side of Smithybridge Station. Four persons, including the driver of the Express were killed and many injured. Rescuers were badly hampered by blizzard conditions and the danger of fire from escaping gas - used to light the carraiges

45

From the records it seems that January was usually the worst month although in 1929 the lake was frozen solid from early March to Easter when special means were used to break the surface. January to February 1902, January 1907, January 1924 and recently in 1941 and 1947 it was frozen following heavy snowfalls.

The effect of wind and storm is very vivid spraying across the roads, over the banks, with all boats securely fastened and the lake looking like an inland sea. On one occasion waves, which were estimated to have risen 20 feet above the normal level, broke the embankment and sank a steamer at its moorings. Conversely it has been almost dry; in 1934 the stones of the buildings at the lake centre could be seen, owing to the lack of water.

DANCING STAGE, HOLLINGWORTH LAKE.

Sports and pastimes

The lake was for a long period a sporting mecca and the different competitions brought crowds of spectators. There was, as late as the 1870's cockfighting, although it was illegal; in 1877 the Landlord of the Lodge Inn and four others were caught and fined for carrying on this 'sport'. There are some who would say it has never really stopped and if you were 'in the know' you could attend a 'main' (cockfight) at the moorland edge of the lake even in recent years. Footraces were common, usually for bets, also evening runs by local youths started from the Institute at Ealees. In 1897 and 1898 the famous Rochdale Hunt Point to Point, usually held at Bagslate, was raced at Rakewood; Mr J Pillings 'Rodee' winning in 1897 and Mr Heaps 'Elsie' in 1898 whilst the Hunt itself held regular runs through the area until its final days after the Great War.

A great change came when in 1883 legal permission for Sunday boating was obtained; so people who usually worked six days could now spend a Sunday at the Lake, on picnics, walks or trying their skill with the rowing boats. It is interesting that the Lake activities in the last century and at its heyday were attended by huge crowds - 40,000 on one occasion, it was said, but I am inclined to think that these figures were exaggerated.

opposite and below
Crowds enjoying a day out at the Lake Hotel Dancing Stage and Playground, probably a Bank Holiday around the time of the First World War; there are several soldiers in the crowd. The two boats, filled to capacity, are heading back for Lakebank

DANCING STAGE AND PLAYGROUND, HOLLINGWORTH LAKE.

The Lake certainly took on and with the Manchester and Leeds, later Lancashire and Yorkshire, Railway advertising halfday trips from the West Riding and the nearby Lancashire towns' crowds could be seen going up from Littleborough and Smithy Bridge stations every weekend. Even the locals made it a day out as that amusing character in the 'Visit to the Manchester Exhibition' says:

'I'm Sam Sandknocker and I live in Smobridge, about Breckfelt, and all my Loife afore Saturdi aw never bin inforin parts but to Hollingworth water, awve never bin ridin but Smobridg, as you know, is neart' Lake and so aw olez went onshanks gallows'.

[He had never travelled, only to the Lake, and he went there on foot].

Swimming became popular, perhaps helped by Captain Webb's training sessions in the cold Lake in preparation for swimming the English Channel. In 1881 Captain Webb swam against G A Jennings of Tunbridge Wells at the Lake in a 5 hour distance race. 2,000 folk turned out to watch and Webb won with 5 miles 660 yards; Jennings swimming just under 4 miles but finishing in better condition than Webb. The race was held up and down a 110 yard course; 'Sporting Life' reported the event as a monotonous and useless achievement. By 1882 regular competitions were held.

J Finney, a famous Lancashire swimmer raced for a mile against one 'Beckwith' of Manchester for the mile championship and bets, but Beckwith retired not finishing the course and complaining about obstructions. A re-swim was arranged for the next Thursday; thousands gathered but Beckwith did not arrive. Others now challenged Finney and later, Sykes of Dewsbury, Collier of Manchester, Beaumont of Stretford, and Robinson of Leeds all swam in a mile race against Finney who won in 29 minutes 27 seconds. Collier chalienged him again and before a large crowd beat Finney in 28 minutes 19 seconds. This so roused interest that the following year Nuttall, a local favourite, swam at the Lake against McCusker of the USA for the 'World Professional Mile Championship' before some 20,000 people and Nuttall won in 26 minutes 8 seconds. If these crowd figures are anywhere near being accurate then the congestion must have been tremendous.

below
Captain Webb, the celebrated long distance swimmer who competed at the Lake during its heyday as a resort
opposite/below
The ruins of the old Rowing Club Boathouse around 1900. At one time this building had been used as refreshment and billiards rooms for the Lake Hotel. On the far side, behind the steamer can be seen the Lancashire and Yorkshire Hotel, later demolished

The contests were regular features and Billington another Lancashire star held the scene from 1902 to 1914 - including a race against Beatrice Kerr, Australian Women Champion, who used the cold water of the Lake for practice. There were often displays of fancy diving and the local youths tried, and sometimes succeeded, to imitate the star performers. Quite a number of young men swam across but this brought much danger and fatal accidents occured. There were dangers too with the rowing boats. A full scale rescue party in 1896 was set up to save a boy reported drowning. This was found to be a stupid hoax and had many repercusssions. Whilst the rowing club was holding its last race of 1907 a muddle took place, several boats collided and five men were thrown in the Lake including GF Walker, Headmaster of Smithy Bridge School, a very keen oarsman. Luckily all were saved; not so on other times as in the case of a man called Nuttall who capsized a boat in an attempt to kill his wife and child, but was himself drowned and they were saved. In 1927 a 15 year old Rochdale boy O Smith was given the Royal Humane Society Certificate for saving a life. Some years later, in the case of two Littleborough youths, one lost his life trying to save his friend who also drowned.

Many were the reported accidents mostly due to carelessness, lack of rowing ability, lack of knowledge of the Lake and its currents and sometimes by bravado. Mr Stott, the boatman, was reputed to have saved nearly 40 lives when he was boatman at the Lake but he and others could do little when towards the end of the last century over 40 boats and the steamer got involved, 13 people fell overboard and of these B Taylor, J Latham, S Smith and R Richardson of Crompton and W Crossley of Shaw were all drowned at a point where the Lake was said to be 16-17 yards deep.

By the end of the century visions widened with the impact of easier travel, more holidays, railways offering seaside excursions and later the introduction of trips on a 'chara'. Longer holidays were taken and a visit to the Lake became commonplace. The Lake had also, with its many activities lost 'tone'. Drinking and fighting happened often; vulgar side-shows, cheapjacks and the like has spoiled its standards and apart from Easter and Whitsun, when the Fair arrived, the Lake was slowly losing its appeal for the masses. So with the closure of hotels, the burning down of the original Beach Hotel and the end of stunts and shows; by 1914 it was somewhat faded as a holiday resort.

The Pals of 1914

With the coming of the Great War, in 1914, the Lake came alive for a short time. Local people noticed military activities in the area and suddenly thousands of soldiers arrived and set up camp in the Ealees Valley. A sea of tents and lines, horses, vans and military equipment came with the Manchester Regiment ('The Pals'), mostly territorials. The local shops in Littleborough and district and the public houses were alerted and people came up in great crowds to see this wonder. The soldiers often came round the district particularly in Durn area, giving away from their trucks, loaves and tins of corned beef; whilst the soldiers' wives and relations came from Manchester District to see them and often lodged in local houses for one or two nights. 'The Old Duke', the Duke of York pub in Ealees, 'The Red Lion' and 'The Rake' were as busy as the Lake pubs but no one realised the imminent and terrible future which awaited these fine young men. They soon sailed for the War to the Dardenelles and few returned, many being mowed down in the terrible landings from their troopships. The people of Littleborough were completely saddened by this terrible waste of young lives. Many of the soldiers' relatives had made friends here and came for many years as visitors and took the walk 'up Ealees' to visit the site of the camp and then the Lake, and revive memories of a brief but happy period.

Autumn 1914, the Territorial Army camps in the Ealees Valley before leaving England for the War. All the transport appears to be horse-drawn

Recent times

Between the two World Wars life at the Lake went along quietly with the Rowing Club developing and a gradual increase in sailing. Most of the old hotels had gone and only the 'Fishermans' and the 'Beach' eventually remained, used probably more at weekends than other days, the Lake with a number of small rowing and motor boats was still popular for an afternoon out. After 1945 with the coach and later car travel, became people more pleasure conscious and made the Lake popular again with a new type of sailing craft and an upsurge of interest in the Rowing Club. What is now known as a Marina developed near the Beach Hotel where a club house was constructed. The rowing club soon achieved a more than local status, entering Agecroft, York, Lancaster and Chester regattas and also in 1964 held its own regatta with nine main events for eights, pairs and sculls; as per programme 44 heats and finishes took place between 12.45 and 6.30 pm with an entry from 17 clubs including schools. Entry was successfully made at Henley where the traditionals there were asking 'from what part of the USA was Hollingworth Lake?'

One of the notable events of recent years was the launching of 'TS Palatine' at the back of the Lake. This is a cadet training centre opened by Lord Derby for the Navy League and various Port Authorities. It cost over £7,000, raised by voluntary subscription, and is used as a weekend or weekly centre for training cadets and youth groups in the Manchester area; basically in pulling, sculling and seamanship. The building has sleeping and recreation facilities with toilets and a galley. At the opening, Leslie Lever MP appealed for support and defined its use after he and Lord Derby had

In 1976 crowds gathered at the Lake to enjoy the long hot summer

been welcomed to Hollingworth by the local Council Chairman AW Colligan JP. It is now fulfilling its intended expectations in providing outdoor activities for youth.

Today, Hollingworth Lake is also a **residential** area. Following the gradual building of Private and Council houses over the last 30 years or so; there has been a great spate of new house building in very recent years on land behind Lake Bank right down towards Smithybridge, and also on the land between the Lake and Milnrow Road. Modern public transport and car ownership means that many people can now work in Manchester or further afield and enjoy the benefits of living on the edge of fine moors and countryside.

The Lake area now has an excellent variety of activities, Sailing Club; Rowing Club; Angling Society; Sub-aqua Group; Caravan site; Rowing Boats; Natural History Group and spaces for people to do nothing at all. An attempt some years ago to put speedboats on the Lake was soon stopped. Just away from the Lake in Rakewood Village is another very recent development - the Rochdalians Sports Area with clubhouse, cricket, rugby and nearly every sport for the youth backed by a Ladies section who organise social functions in the clubhouses.

All these activities, with the natural beautiful surroundings make this lake, constructed nearly 200 years ago to supply water for the new canal, an admirable centre for the proposed Country Park.

below
The bottom of the road up to Hollingworth Fold 1976; with the Motorway viaduct in the distance
opposite/above
Looking down on the Lake from Hollingworth Fold 1976
opposite/below
Hollingworth Fold Cottage 1976. The lintol over the doorway has an inscription 'IMF 1727'

The Country Park

The popularity of Hollingworth Lake and the surrounding area grew steadily, until in December 1971, prompted by Littleborough Civic Trust, a working party was set up to consider the lake's future. Officers of Lancashire County Council, Rochdale Borough Council, Littleborough and Milnrow Urban District Councils and West Pennine Water Board took part in the exercise. Its aim was to assess the recreational potential of Hollingworth Lake. From this it went on to propose the designation of the area as a Country Park and plan its development.

Shortly afterwards Greater Manchester Council was established and took an interest in setting up areas for recreation and leisure such as River Valleys and Country Parks. Fortunately for Hollingworth Lake, at the same time, the Countryside Commission was beginning to support sites close to urban areas. This was particularly important to Hollingworth Lake which was becoming increasingly popular and suffering from overuse, as it meant that there was money available to support the maintenance and development of the new Country Park.

Car parking and traffic management were an obvious problem, and other services - such as toilets, catering and visitor facilities were in limited supply. One of the most controversial decisions at the time was to exclude cars from driving all the way around the lake. This caused a lot of bad feelings among visitors who had, until then, had free if congested

The visitor centre

access to the back of the lake. To compensate for this restriction additional car parks were provided; notably in the Ealees Valley. Domestic rubbish had been tipped in the valley for a number of years prior to 1974. On completion the area was landscaped to create a car park with trees, picnic areas and the Visitor Centre. This Centre had toilet and cafeteria facilities and a limited amount of space for displays and items for sale. A building of similar design was also built on the far side of the lake - known as the Pavilion.

The marshy area at the eastern end of the lake, where the Longden End Brook enters, was made into a nature reserve. Ducks, geese, waders and other birds find this an ideal place to inhabit. Many birds nest in the shelter of the reserve, while others visit for brief periods during the year. One of the rarest visitors in recent years was a collared pratincole, from the Mediterranean, which attracted birdwatchers from far and wide to Hollingworth Lake anxious to catch a glimpse of this unusual shorebird.

The Country Park needed staff to "look after it" and so George Garlick was duly appointed as the Chief Warden in 1974. He was soon to be assisted by another Warden, two Rangers' whose role was to carry out the practical tasks, and two Information Assistants, to staff the Visitor Centre. These staff were responsible for the boating activities on the lake and the bailiffing of the fishing, as well as the development of the area for visitors wanting to enjoy the countryside for walking, picnicking or just relaxing.

The popularity of the area continued to grow steadily and over the years extra staff were employed and additional facilities provided. An extension to the Visitor Centre, completed in 1985, provided both permanent and temporary exhibition areas, a theatre with a slide show about the lake and a mural by local

The Lake is drained for repairs

The scene from Lakebank, 1995. The same viewpoint is seen on page 2, one hundred years earlier

artist Walter Kershaw. This painting, which is about 30 feet long, gives impressions of the lake and the surrounding area from Victorian Times to the present day, and includes many examples of the local wildlife, buildings and activities to be found. Visitors to the Centre increased from 30,000 in 1977, when the building was first opened to the current annual figure of around 130,000. The Country Park staff now provide a full programme of events and activities for visitors, to help them appreciate, understand and enjoy the lake and its surroundings. These include walks led by local experts, childrens' events, both for visiting school parties and weekend and holiday activities, conservation tasks for the enthusiastic, as well as craft days, exhibitions and other entertainment for the casual visitor.

"Draining the Lake"

In 1985 a major event in the history of the lake took place. In that year the lake was drained to carry out repairs to the dams. Under the Reservoirs (Safety Provisions) Act, 1930, all reservoirs had to be inspected and work carried out to bring them up to the standard required. In 1985 it was Hollingworth Lake's turn to be repaired.

Since Hollingworth Lake is not a drinking supply reservoir, there was some debate about whether to carry out the repairs or drain the lake permanently, as they did with Lower Chelburn, at Summit. If the repairs were to be done then a considerable sum of money had to be found before work could commence. The primary source of funding came from North West Water, with contributions from Greater Manchester Council, European Regional Development Funding from the EEC, and Rochdale Metropolitan Borough Council.

To carry out the repairs the water level was dropped, permitting access to the dam banks. Sufficient water remained to allow the fish stocks to survive. The situation was carefully monitored in case oxygen levels became depleted to such an extent that it would endanger the health of the fish. Fortunately, a poor summer ensured this was not the case.

To strengthen the dams, material ranging in size from large boulders to relatively fine gravel was deposited on the dam banks. At the same time the overflow, near Hollingworth Fold, was enlarged and a new spillway and bridge was built so that it was capable of catering with a flood which might occur

once in a thousand years. The "draw off" tower on the Lakebank, which controls the supply of water to the Rochdale Canal was also rebuilt and modernised.

While this work was going on the water based sports - the Rowing Club, the Sailing Club, Sea Cadets from TS Palatine and the sailboarders moved their activities up to Watergrove Reservoir near Wardle Village, approximately four miles away. On completion of the repairs to Hollingworth Lake the sailboarders stayed at Watergrove, but the other clubs returned to their original homeground.

Watergrove is now being developed as an area for recreation and wildlife. As well as footpaths being improved for the visiting public, the area is also being transformed by tree planting schemes, the creation and re-creation of ponds and lodges, the planting of wildflower meadows, and the development of wet areas providing a more varied home for wildlife. Watergrove too has benefited from European funding in the form of grants given to improve the areas appeal to certain species of birds. Watergrove, named after the village that lies beneath the reservoir, contains many interesting historical remains which combined with the enrichment of its wildlife make it a fascinating place to visit.

Back at Hollingworth Lake, the outcome of the upheaval during the repairs was a restored facility, with some notable alterations and improvements. The top water level is now a metre lower than previously, providing room on the lakeside for a promenade between the boathouse and the Fisherman's Inn. This allows visitors the opportunity of strolling close to the waters' edge, without the fear of being run over by passing traffic. An improved sluice system at the eastern end of the lake created lagoons in the nature reserve, which retain water even when the lake level drops dramatically during dry summers. Subsequently, the Countryside Rangers have constructed a bird hide to allow visitors a closer look at the birds in the nature reserve and on the lake.

This brief period in the history of Hollingworth Lake attracted the curious, who were anxious to discover what really was at the bottom of the lake, and to see the work that was going on.

Water Activities

Hollingworth Lake today, just as in the past, provides many people with the opportunity of taking part in water sports and pastimes.

**Looking towards
Blackstone Edge**

Local inhabitants

It's great to be young!

A festive weekend with the morris-dancers, taking part in the annual Rushbearing Festival

The Rowing Club is still going strong after more than a hundred years. Members train all year round and regattas are held, when other clubs are invited to compete against them.

The Sailing Club too has grown in popularity since it was founded in 1946. The club really took off with the advent of the "Firefly" - one of the first post war dinghies. GP14 and Merlin Rockets are now included in the current racing fleet, along with the Firefly. These are joined by Optimist, 405, and Mirror Class dinghies for regular races on Sundays and Wednesday evenings during the summer months. All this activity contributes to the atmosphere - the lake on race days is a fine sight!

On the southern shore of the lake the Sea Cadet base - TS (Training Ship) Palatine - has expanded considerably over recent years. It continues to provide opportunities for youth from both the local area and further afield to learn basic seamanship and navigation skills.

The latest arrival on the lake scene is the Water Activity Centre, developed and run by Rochdale Metropolitan Borough Council. This purpose built centre provides courses in sailing, rowing, sailboarding and canoeing, as well as organising fun events and hiring out craft and equipment. It also now operates the fleet of hire craft, including running the launch the "Lady Alice", giving everybody the opportunity of taking to the water in some way or other.

Fishing is still a popular activity open to all. Matches are held on a regular basis, with the *Rochdale Observer Match* as the premier event of the year, when over 80 anglers take part. Pike over 20 pounds in weight are frequently caught by anglers, along with the more usual catch of carp, tench, roach, bream and perch.

The surprising thing about Hollingworth Lake is that all these activities take place with very little disharmony. Even the ducks and geese stay to entertain the visitors!

The future

It is now over 200 years since the fields at Hollingworth were flooded to create the man made reservoir, which has since become known to everyone simply as "the Lake". With the renewed interest in the Rochdale Canal and the endeavours being put in to return boats to this Pennine route, who knows what the future will bring.

All aboard "The Lady Alice"

Sources and books consulted

Aikin - 40 Miles Around Manchester 1795
Sutcliffe - A Treatise on Canals and Reservoirs 1816
Beckett - A History of The Rochdale Canal 1956
Davenports - Guide to the Lake 1860 et seq
Worralls - Directory various years 1872 et seq
Fishwicks - History of the Parish of Rochdale 1889
Heape - Dated Stones 1926
Robertson - Rochdale Guide and others
Collins - Roof of Lancashire
Royds - Abbots Knowl, A Victorian Story
Healey - Some Good Days with the Rochdale Hunt
Raines - Notita Cestrensis
Raines - Manor of Rochdale
Wrigley - Saddleworth - and many others
Littleborough - Civic Trust Report 1972
Rochdale Observer - Many references eg 'Old
        buildings 1924' etc
Rochdale Observer - Walks by HC Collins
Rochdale Times - 1918 Railway Accident,
        Smithybridge
Harry Percival - Notes and Articles in Rochdale
        Observer
Waugh - Sketches of Lancashire Life 1867
Oakley - Olden Days
Mattley/Heywood - Annals of Rochdale
Aspin - Lancashire Life, October 1975

I believe many documents, reports and deeds etc with reference to the Lake area were kept in a trunk at Milnrow Vicarage - Deposited by Canon Raines FSA

Local names in the Hollingworth Lake area
With suggested meanings

Sources
Sephton - Lancashire Place Names
Colley-March - Nomenclature of Rochdale Names
Jackson - Local Notes
Brierley - Adventures amongst words
(Ben) Brierley - Ab-o'th-Yates Dictionary
Collier - Glossary of Words and Phrases
Cunliffe - Glossary of Rochdale and Rossendale Words

Key
OE - Old English
NOR - Norse or Scandinavian
AS - Anglo Saxon
D - Local Dialect

Peanock or pennock
'Pyndan' is AS for penfold or pinfold; to impound also paddock or parrock. So Peanock was the small walled or fenced-round enclosure for cattle.

Clegg, Cleggswood, Clegghall and many variants
Clegg is generally taken to mean clay but in Welsh 'clegr' means a rock but it seems that the reference to clay is the local use.

Ogden
In OE, 'Og' means Oak and 'den' is a valley or dene. The word dale is used more in the north. Ogden is the valley or dean with oaks. Ogden was famous for oak trees but now only small ones can be seen.

Piethorn
Thorn is common for thorn or briar trees. 'Pie' is D for pynot or magpie, so piethorn explains itself.

Blackstone Edge
Can mean just what it says, the border stone on the edge of the moor. It also can come from 'Blacan'. AS to shine or 'Blacea', NOR meaning pale or bleached. At one time the millstone grit surface was grey and shone in the western sun but industrial smut ended that.

Bleaked Hill
One of the small knowls or hills in the Lake area and very exposed so the name comes from early days.

Hollingworth

From 'Hollen' or 'Holen' which in OE meant Holly. Worth came from OE 'weorth', an enclosed homestead. 'ing' came from NOR a meadow in swampy ground, so Hollingworth is enclosures or homesteads near swampy ground where the holly tree grows.

Rakewood

'Rake' is D for track, path or sheepwalk, wood is from OE 'wuda', a wood or forest so Rakewood is the path to the woods.

Booth Hollins

Booth is from N 'buth', a dwelling or distant place in connection with animals. 'Hollins' from Holly. Booth Hollins is the herdman's hut near the holly trees away from the homestead.

Schofield

From 'Scholes' and 'Skali' NOR primary meaning is a hut or shed for a guard or watcher. 'Field', pasture or arable land. Schofield suggests the person living in a building as a guard against raiders, on distant pastures.

Shaw, Shawmoss

Shaw from OE 'sclaga' or AS 'scura' a copse or shady place, 'Moss' is swampy or peat ground. Shawmoss is the small copse or tree area near the swamp.

Syke

From Latin 'siccium' and AS 'sich' or 'sigan', to subside, a summer dried water furrow or rivulet. As a place name means the homestead near the rivulet.

Ealees

'Ea' is AS for water or stream. 'Lees' or 'Lea' is OE for pasture, meadow. Ealees means the meadows by the stream.

Smithy Bridge

There was a smithy near the Old Blue Ball Inn and the bridge.

Abbots Knowl Higher and Lower Abbots

The Abbot of Whalley owned much land in the parish of Rochdale and the Oldham side of the lake could have connection which Roche Abbey. Knowl is a small hill.

Lidiate, Lydgate or Lydiate

All are from OE meaning an opening in wall or fence. In OE 'hlid' means to swing and AS 'Hlidgeat' is opening to castle. "This gate hangs here and hinders none' said the Inn sign at the Lydgate Inn closed in the 1930s.

Antioch, Gilead

These names arise from the influence of the Methodist People and their chapels in Rakewood.

Tandle Hill

In AS the word for fire is 'Tern' or 'Tan'. Tandle though not at the Lake is in the area and was a point for a beacon to warn people of danger, as were Blackstone Edge and similar high points.

Dearnley

Lea or Ley is a pasture or arable land. 'Deora', AS for a personal name. 'Dern' AS secret or private. Dearnley is suggested as secluded pasture or private pasture owned in AS times by Deora.

Whittaker

In OE 'hivit' meant fair and white; 'Aecer' is in AS a measure of corn land (hence acre) 'Hwita' is also a personal AS name. Whittaker could thus be the land owned by one Hwita or the name given because of the white aspect when the land was full of corn.

These old tickets for the Hollingworth Lake Ferry Boats were discovered about 1960, in the premises of J B Edmondsons of Cheetham Manchester shortly before they closed down. Edmondsons were the designers and makers of all the early railway ticket and fare collection systems. These tickets for boats date from 1867 - 1872 when the Lake was at its height as a pleasure resort. Manuscript instructions on the back of the tickets show that they were ordered in tens of thousands from the printers.

From the collection of David Kaiserman

below

A quiet day at the Lake around 1900; looking towards the Fisherman's. The road seems to be unmade and the drystone wall around the bank has not yet been built